Knowing is a Branching Trail

**Winner of The Birdy Poetry Prize—2021
by Meadowlark Press**

Knowing is a Branching Trail

Alison Hicks

Emporia, Kansas, USA

Meadowlark Press, LLC
meadowlark-books.com
P.O. Box 333, Emporia, KS 66801

Knowing Is a Branching Trail
Copyright © Alison Hicks, 2021

Cover Image: "Ediacaran fossils Mistaken Point Newfoundland.jpg" by Alicejmichel is licensed under CC BY-SA 4.0. Modifications were made to the original image. https://creativecommons.org/licenses/by-sa/4.0/deed.en

Interior Design: TMS, Meadowlark Press

All rights reserved. This book or any portion thereof may not be reproduced or used in any manner whatsoever without the express written permission of the author except for the use of brief quotations in a book review.

POETRY / Women Authors
POETRY / Subjects & Themes / General
POETRY / American / General

Library of Congress Control Number: 2021943450

ISBN: 978-1-7362232-6-0

For Charlie and Jeremy

Also by Alison Hicks

Poetry:
You Who Took the Boat Out
Unsolicited Press, 2017

Kiss
PS Books, 2011

Falling Dreams
Finishing Line Press, 2006

Fiction:
Love: A Story of Images
Amherst Writers & Artists Press, 2004

Anthology:
*Prompted: Stories, Poems, Essays
from Greater Philadelphia Wordshop Studio*,
edited with Elizabeth Mosier and Thérèse Halscheid
PS Books, 2010

Table of Contents

We Could Say It's Like This

Island 3
The Pursuit 4
The Moon Is a Paper Lantern, Arm of the Boy
    Who Carries It Tired.. 5
Poem Ending with Lines by Samuel Beckett 6
Suites for Solo Cello, May 2020 7
The Front Room 8
Vigil 9
Groundwater 10
Oneself 11
From a Prescribed Distance 12
Margaret Atwood in Quarantine 13
An Open Door Is an Invitation
    in the Same Way as a Closed Box 14
Night After Eclipse 16
Buciumeana 17
Bartók 18
Bartók in America 19
The Task... 20
Knowing Is a Branching Trail
    that Disappears into Variety 21
Walking the Dog I 22
Walking the Dog II 23
Twin 24
Lives of Trees 25
Starlings 26
The Pelicans 28
Sea Otter 29
Oakmont 30
We Could Say It's Like This 31
Landscape with Citrus 33
Who Is Right About Moonlight? 34
The Aurochs 35

How It Is
Yellow Bird 39
Boat 40
Riffles 41
Sunflower 43
Katydids & Cicadas 44
How It Is 45
The Winter Magician 46
Pain in the Neck 47
St. Peter's Shadow 48
Migraineurs 50
Heart, Lungs, Bladder 51
Color 52
The IV Pole 53
Westland House 54
My Mother in Fall 56
Overpass 57
Grass 58
Eighteen Lines for a Young Life 59
Untitled 60
North Pacific 61
In Winter 62
To My Son 63
Flatirons 64
Calls 65
Letter to the Sky 67
Practice 68
Branch 69
The Cup 70
Understanding 71

Notes 75
About the Author 79
Acknowledgments 81
Publication Credits 83

We Could Say It's Like This

Island

To have a skin loose enough to shake
is something to aspire to.
The dog carries his clothing on his person.
Everything he needs except traffic sense.
Every time you walk out the door
you're making a prediction.

In the bowl of your hands
water drains through.
Leaving the bean, the seed,
flower that in the hand blooms
then dies.

On the other side of the ocean
trees bear oranges and coconuts,
bougainvillea climbs.
A bird is flying.
Sun coming out of clouds.

The Pursuit

vivid in the moment of waking
has broken up, pieces scattered and hidden.

They may be found anywhere.
You hold one in your hand.

A stone in the middle of a river,
lip of water passes.

Listen, crouch in the reeds.

Join one to another. Lay it down.

The Moon Is a Paper Lantern, Arm of the Boy Who Carries It Tired

I used to find my dog's hair in birds' nests,
soft layer woven inside the twigs.
I release hair from my hairbrush out my bedroom window.

My son practices "The Swan" transposed for viola.
Shift to third position, then to fifth.
*You want to hear just a bit of the slide,
near the end of the note,* his teacher says.
Don't touch the neck. The hand moves as a unit.

*String instruments, where pitch is found by memory,
offer the most choices for musicality,
are the most expressive, most like the voice.*

I print out the music, finger the notes on my forearm.
You have to have a plan, Mr. Barnett says.
I haven't touched the cello in months.

The house is large, the ceilings high.
I run from room to room
laughing at the sound of my shoes.
No one is dancing, only me, twirling on the wooden floor.

Poem Ending with Lines by Samuel Beckett

What remedy for loss of singing,
with others, together in an enclosed space, a sanctuary?

Not that I was any good at it. Nature made me alto,
preference bass, an octave higher.

Listen, put me next to anyone, I'll follow their pitch.
Useless in a choir.

Still, eighty percent of the point of church to me is song.
The rest should be silence, in my mind.

I used to go to Quaker Meeting.
And once to Russian Orthodox Easter:

clouds of smoke from the swinging thurible,
Znamenny chant,

church going dark
at midnight, the slow illumination,
touching wick to wick.

So you must not think of certain things, of those that
      are dear to you,
or rather you must think of them . . .

Suites for Solo Cello, May 2020

I didn't know how I'd crave it, black and long like a bar,

taking a stool, fingers dropping onto strings, lining up
    shots of sound.

At fifteen, in France, I bought three records, Pablo Casals
    playing Bach.

Packed them in the bottom of my suitcase for the journey
    home.

Never thought I'd put the instrument down.

When I did, I didn't expect it would be thirty years before
    I picked it up again,

that three hundred years after they were written I'd
    clamber to drink in those Suites,

requisite movements, fingers stiffened through variation,
repetition.

The Front Room

A light is on in the room in the front
across from our bedroom on the second floor,
where in the daytime Chloe practices violin.
This has to do, I think, with Joe, her father,
diagnosed with leukemia.
The transplant he was supposed to have this spring
postponed, the rounds of chemo not.
Maybe like me he is resisting sleep,
these nights I stay up too late
reading more of what I already know
will not make a difference.
Something will not resolve
though I pretend:
if I stay up, if I keep reading
if the light stays on.

Vigil

In India there's a *Rag* for every hour,
when in the west the last notes of the service
have faded into stone and the Great Silence re-descends,
relieving monks and the few awake
of the burden of speaking.

Kin stationed by bedsides,
determined to wait out the night.
A new mother, child at her breast,
chilled by the open window as summer turns to fall.
Insomniacs twisting in sweated sheets.
Migraineurs wakened by a dream of pain.

Hours of improvisation,
silent as wings of owl,
paws imprinting snow,
sitar the air, calling to sunrise.

Groundwater

channels under structures—
cities, cathedrals, parking lots—
streams over asphalt, seeking the drain,

always somewhere to move,
a path carved,

groove to fall into.

One yard's trouble empties into the next,
pumped into streets where it runs off,

splashed onto feet and tires, carried home on shoes.

It starts in the snowpack, a crack
through which it drips, rolls downhill, gathering its kind.

Oneself

A woman and a man newly in love
were sailing across the Pacific.
In a storm he was thrown overboard.
She hallucinated his presence,
drifting for forty-one days before finding land.

My best singing is done alone.
In a car, while washing the dishes.
Along with the radio, to a tune in the head,
made up even better.

In a café, small table by oneself
watching the rest of the tables fill up and empty.
Acid and foam against the lip,
no need for performance,
to compose a face and arrange thoughts.

Once she was awakened by stadium lights
shining through night, a ship too large
to make out the crippled yacht
with broken mast and makeshift sail.
Flares could not reach as high as its deck.
It steamed right past.

From a Prescribed Distance

Everybody's looking, watching to see
what everyone else is doing.
Waiting for the slip, the error.
So easy to make, new actions not yet routine.
Outrage and satisfaction of witness.
Who was that unmasked man?
Who took the last container of wipes,
threw down gloves in the parking lot?
Who blocked the aisle, went down the wrong way?
Is it possible to go around and come back
to make it right or is the insult impossible
to remove? Calculating the odds of distances.
How many of these folks are shopping for themselves?
How many are mercenaries, sent to fetch a list?
Who coughed in their bed last night?
Who runs a secret fever?

Margaret Atwood in Quarantine

Lean up against its side, push it open like the flap
    of a cardboard box,
burrow deep into the present:
whatever you find there on the other side
won't be the future you're forced to live through,
that bad movie where the exits are sealed and
    have no give,
the world you must make your peace in.

While Fiction, a witness less baroque than Truth,
pleads the case for the chain of events it has rendered
    into motion,
I sneak out of the courtroom, go back and push
on another flap of that box, finding myself somewhere
    else.

An Open Door Is an Invitation in the Same Way as a Closed Box

1. The troubles had been packed in
   squished against each other
   so thick they could hardly breathe.
   At that moment, the lid opened
   and air rushed in.

2. During their time in the box
   the troubles had forgotten
   what it was like outside.
   They huddled together on the sidewalk, homeless.

3. One of them saw a person pass by and jumped.
   From his perch
   he waved at the other troubles
   standing there wringing their hands.

4. The man was coming home from work.
   He felt a weight
   that he didn't remember from that morning.
   A bad day, he thought.

5. The other troubles scattered
   in search of people.
   Once they looked around
   there was no shortage.
   It was easy to jump
   onto a swaying arm or leg
   a piece of clothing
   or catch a foot or toe
   hoist up from there.

6. The troubles liked to climb
   as far up as possible.
   It seemed strange to them
   that people didn't brush them off.

That's how they discovered
they were invisible.

7. They found they could survive
   on the crumbs of what people ate.

8. In time people became so used
   to carrying troubles around
   that they couldn't remember
   a time when they hadn't.

9. They grew bonded.
   So when a trouble was removed
   when it fell or was scraped
   off by circumstance
   people felt they had lost something
   and mourned.

Night After Eclipse

Dot on a giant exclamation point
the moon sitting at the end of my street.

What does it mean to tell me,
what message does it punctuate?

Toss away the chatter and take this body
that orbits our planet, whom we have visited,
but know little about, for which we have questions
that slice through the skin like a paper cut.

Last night it was eclipsed,
rolling through the shadow of our planet.
Two times I stepped out on the porch to see it,
as small then and high up as it is large and low tonight,
watercolored red, uneven and streaked.

A friend told me that she mixed up the days,
wondered why she was the only one staring up,
wanting to call out to everyone to come and see.
The moon, remarkable as it always is.

I remembered that the sun is closest to earth in winter,
how passing close to a source of light
we are distant, staring into the universe.
Light-years away,
we may seem less so face to face.

Buciumeana

Violin in my heart
bow off the string
winding semitones
up the A string

river running under stone

when we are quiet enough

to hear can never be unlearned

Bartók

In the afternoon dark, harvest time,
the road covered with leaves,
the stranger with the wax cylinders
has persuaded the oldest woman in the village to sing.
Melody winds from her throat
out through the fields.
An oompah band is setting up on the green
for the evening's dance.
Chords spill
out church doors.
In the fields,
men and women look up,
wipe faces with their kerchiefs.
Across an ocean
strange intervals carry
shadows of late afternoon.

Bartók in America

Every country has a music
running underneath like blood in veins.
To hear you must descend.
In a country now lost,
I traveled beyond edifices and artifice
to dirt-road villages, and then here,
where I am an exile, a wrapper on a bit of cheese,
discarded among so many others, collecting in the gutter.
The wind blows, and blows us with it.
I miss the strange old songs.
I should have wished to be a peasant in the Magyar
    countryside
when I was a boy, instead of some performer
    pounding on keys.
The music here, of my adopted country,
I can make no sense of it. Like some old married man
my ear has become indifferent,
so finely tuned to one it must forsake all others.
Koussevitzky out of pity offers me a commission.
I accept because it lets me dream
in the tones my ear remembers.

The Task

Late at night into the time before dawn is best.

Too easy to put off in the afternoon—
how long until cocktails, a swim, dinner?

Salvage enough to approach sideways, crab-like.

Lighted by what you wanted,
present what you've lifted proudly,
though it might be refused.

You could be drinking, pouring a mug
to really twist you up.

Instead you're here.

When it is dark it seems like darkness
will go on for a long time.

Even when you go out on the porch to look at the stars.

All of this supposing, of course,
that you are not required to rise early.
Mornings you'll need sleep.

Knowing Is a Branching Trail that Disappears into Variety

It is hard to find something you have not first
    imagined.
Only a small portion of the world is known with
    accuracy, Darwin wrote.

Ediacarans went extinct 541 million years ago.
Their tracks can be seen at Mistaken Point,
    Newfoundland.
They look like a series of parentheses laid inside each
    other.

Soft-bodied, mouth- and anus-less,
    somehow they began to crawl,
pushing disclike bodies forward.

They were hunting or escaping a predator.
We don't know. We're not even sure they were
    animals.
They could have been plants, fungi, or
    colonies of single-celled organisms.

It could have been an accident.
Extending bodies into the stream, washed from their
    perch,

like anemones pried from their rocks, who
    creep across sand to a hard surface,
they might have stretched suction-cup feet
across a gelatin of bacterial mats, working to
    feel their way back.

Walking the Dog I

We go out searching.
He with his nose,
me with my eyes.
He smells what I can't see.

His nostrils take in
all that has happened
close to the ground
since we were last here.

He traces the scent
to the absolute edge of the leaf.
I look for the woodpecker,
locate only the sound,

no body in the branches.
Thwack. A car door closing
startles, makes him jump.
He is afraid of loud noises, thunder.

I am afraid of being wrong
and being yelled at, though I'm as guilty
as anyone else of judging and yelling.
He is guilty of not barking.

In the middle of the night,
he tore up the blinds,
trying to claw his way outside
rather than wake us.

Walking the Dog II

He parcels out the narrative in installments along the
    way:
another day on the rope with my human, heading west.
I had some chicken-flavored breakfast, drank some water.

My electrolytes are basically in balance, all systems go
except the reproductive, which seems to be inactive.
I sleep comfortably on the chair. My humans
    are good that way.

I understand some trade-offs are required. Not that
    I had any say.
Most days I'd prefer to skip the collar, ditch the rope.
When I get a chance I run, kick my back legs up.

I was bred for cross-country travel, to find raccoons
    and trap them in trees.
Here, the raccoons I've been able to track
live underneath the streets.

I get a whiff at the openings, can't reach them or
    lure them to trees.
Squirrels don't count, beneath my notice. Likewise small
    yapping dogs.
I look over at the fuss, walk on. The
    neighborhood fox is a tease.

I leaned on the old fence once, tipped myself
    over and went after him.
Tough on the stomach and I didn't catch him.
My humans take me to the dog park, instruct me to run.

It isn't the same. By now I've sniffed
every millimeter of that perimeter.
I'm sure you've caught a few of my status updates there.

Twin

Our houses share a wall, horsehair plaster from the 1920s
that cures as lime reacts with carbon pulled from air.

>May we too be cured by fibers of belonging
>mixed into the atmosphere in which we're formed.

A pattern of sand and calcite crystals
that hairs from horses' tails made more flexible, less likely to
    crack.

>It helps to be flexible if you live in a twin: to stretch
>   and breathe and laugh.
>Arguments travel easily as cracks.

Living here, we've all made journeys through walls
spread our lives' patterns over old boards,

>squeezed through and out the other side, forming
>   keys,
>as in the original construction, to lock around lath,
>   strong enough to cement

our claims as we step onto mirror-image staircases
suspended from a wall of horsehair plaster from the 20s.

Lives of Trees

The township is cutting down the last big tree on
    Colfax,
whose shade covered two lots and reached
to claim the opposite sidewalk and half a yard.
From my second floor I see a man in the white bucket,
orange vest. His bobbing saw like a toy.

The street has been blocked off two days with orange
    cones.
How many men does it take to bring down
an oak that, rotted from inside, threatens to crush
one or more roofs in the next storm?
In this case, five.

In the forest, this giant would come down of its own
    accord,
smaller trees braking its way to the ground,
where it would be used by insects and spiders,
molds and mosses, broken down
to enrich the soil and feed new plants.

No way here for old trees to die gracefully.
Damage must be contained.
Top branches lopped, fed into the chipper.
Larger chunks lie on the ground.
My husband takes one for a chopping block.
The trunk a sculpture with no arms
they will come back for tomorrow.

Pin oaks planted between sidewalk and street
grow fast but throw less shade
than the big old trees that must have been planted
when the suburb was created, farm by farm,
from land once claimed from forest,
hacked from trees that made their home here first.

Starlings

i.
He was hanging by a leg
from the gutter of our house.
Dead, of course, by the time we noticed.
He must have been scouting for a nest
and somehow his foot caught.
There he stayed, tavern sign or tarot card:
the hanged starling.

ii.
What did it mean? We wanted to know.
How long had it taken for the bird to die?
A human being would have yelled
until someone heard and brought opposable thumbs
to unhook what was caught.
Was he stoic, in the way we expect animals to be,
or had he made a sound we didn't recognize or
      understand?

iii.
It wasn't easy to reach him,
so we let him hang all fall,
and when it got cold,
we came inside and forgot.
In spring, we looked up from the patio,
and he was gone—
loosened with icicles or taken by a squirrel
or hollowed out so much hanging there
that his body blew away.

iv.
Shortly after we'd moved in,
a starling fell down our chimney.
He landed on the hearth, took a couple of jerky steps,
then flew up, full wings
wider and stronger than I expected.

My instinct was to duck, his to fly,
so he made for the stairs,
wing grazing my hair.
He churned the air, beating and thrashing
in that artificially enclosed place:
the shelter we needed, having lost
the fur that had protected us.
(His power, our diminishment.)

v.
Once we gave it some thought,
it wasn't so difficult to get him out.
We turned off the lights in the house,
kept the porch light on.
Then we opened the door.

vi.
We had a wire grate placed over the chimney.
Sometimes they nest outside my office,
in the space between the air conditioner
and the windowsill. They make a song,
that isn't quite song—a low coo-trill
that enters under
the threshold of my hearing.

The Pelicans

You could be swimming along minding your own
when the shock from that body hits. Watch out, fish.
Now that these flyboys are back,

they live to tuck and drill down.
They'll scoop you up, hinge back their gullets,
snap them shut on a trip you're not coming back from.

Pelicans fly low up the coast
in formation, with few strokes,
heads back, scanning the waves.

They used to fly into Fisherman's Wharf for R and R
until the authorities chased them off.
Rougher and larger close up, lounging on the railings,

strutting in their battered jackets,
peering down their oversized beaks
at the crowds gathered to get a look at the outlaws.

Sea Otter

Thicker than seal, denser than mink,
the fur for which you hunted us almost to extinction.

You celebrate our survival as your success,
stuff fabric likenesses for your young.

Approaching our rafts, you judge our lives
   undemanding;
how pleasant to wrap oneself in kelp and ride the
   waves.

You forget our sharp teeth and our drudgery.
Our omnivore metabolism's drive.

We carry no blubber, less body fat than you.
We must dive and dive and dive.

A quarter of our body weight a day, consumed.
Squid, abalone, urchin, whatever we can find.

And after, groom, each hair precisely arrayed.
Skin exposed is death.

We've been to the bottom and felt its offerings.
We, like you, must surface.

Oakmont

First comes the marking of the trunk
with a fluorescent pink or orange *X*,
followed sometime later by a town crew,
men with trucks and ropes and saws who put in a day's work,
two at most, leave hollowed-out stumps
of what we assumed solid all the way through.

Minus the canopy, the streets seem more open,
less mysterious and otherworldly.
Still, it's restful to walk with a dog in the evening through
    lesser foliage.
Some have taken to planting flowers and decorative
    grasses
in the strip of township land between sidewalk and
    pavement.
Watch for pavers lifted and tilted by roots.

Dutch Colonials: how many years before I learned
to discern the basic shape through disguises:
eaves-front gambrel roof beneath pushed-out
    dormers,
enclosed front porch hiding the chimney?
Myths to explain where we are.

We Could Say It's Like This

The time I was cooling off in the Tye,
and decided to swim down to the confluence with the James
because I wanted to see what it looked like
where the one flowed out into the other.
August, and the water at its deepest barely reached
    my waist.
I part-crawled, part-strode, part-floated.
It was not a long way, but felt longer than I'd thought
to pass under the railroad bridge. Still I was game.
On the banks, fields with cows, swishing their tails, lowing.
I never got there. When I reached the flat, open space
    on the right
that suggested I was close, thunder and a dark cloud at the
    edge of the sky
commanded that I turn around.
Going back, I had to push against the current.
It proved fastest to crawl, water cresting around my body,
annoyed at the resistance I was providing.
Did I think of you, co-conspirators,
companions on parallel journeys it is necessary to
    undertake alone,
that we may reconstruct for each other afterwards?
I could see the railroad bridge.
Now I was breathing in deep gasps,
grabbing hold of rocks with my feet and hands
to keep myself from being swept back.
I needed to be out of the water before the storm
    caught up to me.
A guest in this country, I would be trespassing
were I to step out onto land where I had not been invited.
By the time I reached the wooden dock sticking out into mud,
it had started to rain. Moving toward it, my ankles sank.
I pulled myself up, shorts over my dripping suit, my towel
    around me,
muscles trembling, walking as fast as I could,
panting up the road, the turn up the hill,
counting seconds between rumbles,

arriving finally at the house where I was staying,
the room on the second floor
and the porch that looks down on the James,
invisible through trees in this season,
a dip in the green before the hillside rising on the
    other side,
the river that I've known is there and never seen.

Landscape with Citrus

The winter she was thirsty
oranges cut the paste in her mouth.
Digging fingernails into the rind,
peeling slices from the bitter white,
sucking juice.

It rained and it snowed and rained again.
The oil left fragrance on her fingers.
She was still thirsty.

Tides were higher.
Waves chipped at the land.
Fruit rotted on the tree.
She drank water but it didn't penetrate.
She was thirsty and there were no oranges.

Who Is Right About Moonlight?

I.
The facts are simple:
It rises and sets every day at a different time,
in constant cycles of increase, diminishment.

You don't have to stay up late or get up early.
Going about your business, look up in full sunlight.
It might be hanging there, dim-shadowed shape.
And even if you know why and how this happens,
it's startling for that moment
seeing it where it doesn't seem to belong.

II.
When my father sang "There's a Long, Long Trail,"
I'd see the path switchbacking up the mountain.
Ryōkan woke and saw the thief. He felt rich,
ran after him with the cushion he'd forgotten to steal.
He could not give him the moon in his window,
the beam that shone through the timbers of Izumi
    Shikibu's hut.
Dogen spoke of reflection in which the moon does not get
    wet,
nor the water broken.

Waxy flowers in the desert bloom one night a year.

The Aurochs

I had been kept in darkness,
had not eaten in some days.
When they brought me out into the hall,
men were feeding the blaze on the floor.
It hurt my eyes; I squinted, turned away.

They gave me the drink. I climbed up,
lay on my back on the frame they had constructed.
Light traveled, unfolding over stone.
I reached my hand to meet the wall and waited.

They showed themselves first as tremors
barely detectable below my fingers,
growing as they came on,
until the sound of their hooves was a roar.

I stretched to brush their flanks
and as they passed they became visible to me,
and I marked them as they came on, their pendant
    bellies,
tapered horns, their noses, knobby legs.

They ran through the rock.
To make others see, I marked them.

How It Is

Yellow Bird

I want to believe in a world beneath this one.
The bird that flies across the lawn
is a messenger, that if I follow her
in my mind, I will come to a door.
She will let me through to the underside of the world.
I will look at my life from below,
my husband and son walking,
the bottom of their shoes.

Other times I think there is no door, nothing below.
The bird flying bent on her own purposes,
her color the outcome of natural selection.
Nothing mystical, just the world working itself out.

Hummingbirds are squeaking, dive-bombing the feeder.
I, too, sitting right-side up in this world.
The bird keeps coming back.
The bird speaking through me.

Boat

Who would have carried it this far,
up the crest between watersheds,
then quit before the downhill?

It doesn't seem old enough
to have been stranded
when this land was covered
by shallow waters

that buckled and rose,
dividing the water.
Every year it sheds a board.
The paint muted,

drawn into surrounding foliage.
If the trees know the story, they aren't saying.
A trunk has pushed through the hull
pinning the bow to the hillside.

So it can hardly be the lifeboat
we will step into
when the waters fill the valley again
that will allow us to float away.

Riffles

Midsummer

The whole nightmoon
three days off full
katydids
all to myself

Sense

It's not supposed to
the pattern of clouds
on a cool June day
the way things fall
in place or not
you give them
sense they don't have
to make and things
happen no matter
how many times
you crossed/uncrossed
or rubbed the stone

Beach

The hole you've dug
deep enough to see the waves

Turning Down

Slow turning down
end of day
if you hike
in the late afternoon
through the pines
maybe in snow

you might not even notice
the dimming until lavender
appears above gray

Stream

Melting into the stream
little fishes come & nibble
can something be caught twice
once a subject is chosen
is it possible to write
of the same thing again?

Sunflower

The bloom becomes too heavy
after a season of moving toward the sun,
the face turns down, trains on the earth
from which nourishment no longer rises.
By the time the birds have lightened the burden,
the neck, dry with bending,
touches the pavement.
Presses its ear to the place it grew away from,
to the scuttle of creatures that sleep in its roots.

Katydids & Cicadas

When did they stop?
More rain, afterward a cool wind.
I did not notice when they went.
Evenings by the firepit,
crickets scrape their wings in time
to changing air.

How It Is

The white car that lives in the white of the eye
comes out of the sun
behind the line of parked cars,
the potted plant on the corner.

Always there, travels submarine.
Hides in white blood cells,
cruises arteries and veins,
slides through the body politic.

All the times it hasn't shown
you've sensed its filmy existence,
so never completely a surprise
when it surfaces in peripheral vision.

The white car could be an actual car.
It could be an election,
getting lost in the woods for five days and nights,
a birth or death.

Too late to hit the gas, to swerve,
always your fault.
Tuck your head as it pulls you down,
slide through until it stops.

The Winter Magician

makes earth hard and turns rain white.
He lives in a cave and doesn't care
to perform tricks of resurrection or resurgence.

His audience is captive.
He pointedly ignores them as he goes about his business,
building a parsimonious fire.

His blood is slow to rise,
his fingers never truly warm.
Pain his only assistant, not lovely in the least.

After his meal of watery rabbit stew,
eaten with a bent spoon,
they converse.

Sometimes he brings out the deck and she picks a card.
Always the same one.
He still won't tell her how he does it.

He works methodically:
given one season to reveal the bones,
he does no more, no less.

Pain in the Neck

Crick traveling down

Hitch in the latch

Muscles ticktock

Won't be kneaded & needled out
stretched, medicated
into submission

Tunnels into tissue deeper
where memory adds to its minefield

Animal's instinctive tensing

First to take the hit

In a building that never burns
fire alarm ringing

Waiting for the flame
to catch & spread

St. Peter's Shadow

The sick studied St. Peter's movements,
anticipating the hour and the angle of the sun,
the wall against which his shadow would fall
so it would fall onto them, and they would be cured.

Scrambling for the right place at the right time
on inadequate limbs, or with markings on the skin,
or maladies not so obvious, demons inside
    chewing on the wires.

Remember the people who got on the bus for
    Mexico and laetrile?
A few years ago, it was announced in my yoga class
that a Chinese doctor was coming.
If we wanted to see him, we could go into the city and
    wait.

I thought about it, I really did.
This man might have draped his fingers over my skull,
smoothed down my brain, coaxed the pain out.

Perhaps, after studying my urine,
he would make me drink a sticky goo
I would barely be able to choke down,
the way the healer in Tibet cured my friend's
    daughter's foot.

The body wants healing, cries out for it,
child pulling incessantly on her mother's arm.
I didn't go.

I take my preventives and my rescues.
The doctors say it won't kill you,
as if dying's what you're worried about.

When you run out of meds, or they don't work—
the times you ride it out, those you remember,

how in the passenger seat from Columbus to
 Philadelphia
with a clutch of plastic bags, you threw up every few
 miles.
Or the time on vacation, it lasted five days, no
 medicine would touch it.

How you survived, and how relieved you were when it
 broke.
To have a condition is to give yourself over
to hands not your own, or even human.

Migraineurs

We are an ancient order, like epileptics or diabetics,
though there are more of us.
No one can account for our existence,
nor the increase in our numbers,
except by reproductive or survival advantage.

It might have been good for the tribe
to have some individuals lie down for a period of time
in the back of the cave, out of the light.

Did we survive when the rest were picked off?
Our brains sang changes like whales
dropping to the deep. If there was error in our design
it might have been useful, for spiritual reasons, to
    excuse a few
from the routines of maintaining physical life.

Our kind counted among shamans,
the first to have time thrust upon us:
sickness turned to gift,
painting animals on the walls,
calling down their properties for deliverance.

Painting spears piercing the sides of animals,

as we may have wished for the flint
to score hairline to nose,
peel back the skin, release the spirit
who sent visions and fed us strings of words
we whispered to distract ourselves from pain,
to call the animal to us for the kill.

Heart, Lungs, Bladder

The body is a container that leaks.
Skeleton a cage
from which to build shelter.
Where is the line between inner and outer?

Kidney, liver, gall bladder:
in Chinese medicine
organs of purification.
Separating what to let
pass through.

Water we hold in our hands
drips down our fingers.
We hold thoughts for as long as we can
before they pass out of us.

We contain feelings
when they have power.

Contain to protect.

We have devised many structures:
jails, prisons, hospitals,
barriers, ropes, lines of armored police
with helmets, clubs, tear gas and guns.

Schools and gated communities.

Containment is not the same as holding.
What we hold passes through us
on to others, gift or curse.

Perfume escapes the bottle
slowly through threads.

Neurons fire across a gap.

Color

In the salon, a woman's head is being rubbed with
    lavender foam.
Her legs stick out under the cape,
identical to those of the woman next to her, veined and
    putty-like.
Old lady day here. It always is.
Something to do, it seems, go to the salon and have your
    hair done.
Hers so white it's translucent underwater; her crown
    looks bald.
At the doctor's, everyone asks, *You still having periods?*
The gynecologist says, *You aren't the oldest. I have a
    patient,*
didn't go into menopause until sixty.
My hairdresser says, *That boy giving you gray hairs,*
asks if it's time to talk about color.
When I've projected into the future,
I've seen myself with shoulder-length white hair.
I tell her I haven't made up my mind.
You'll have to make a decision soon, she says.
You know, so it won't be obvious.
I admit I hadn't thought of that.

The IV Pole

watches over bodies more fragile than itself
through nights that are never dark and always interrupted.
Sentry, dripping saline, sedatives, antibiotics,

accepting all bags hung on it
as it accepts all patients it is wedded to by tube and blood,
calibrated to needs not its own,

to a number that commands
injection that makes eyes grow soft
and pain a stream easily stepped over.

It has danced with every partner it's hooked up with.
Roller-slide and grip-slipper step to the bathroom,
tubing grapevining around appendages.

When it passes its fellows in the hall, protocol excludes
    open recognition.
If all the poles in the unit were to be brought together,
would they jostle, bump antler tops?

When the bags run out, when an arm kinks and flow is
    disrupted,
it calls with a sound no one cares to hear.

Westland House

From the glass door in my father's room
we watched the acorn woodpecker
hopping up and down the trunk of the pine.
Anne had brought birdseed, stored it behind the door.

We admired him. I was nervous about the visit,
afraid of Anne. I didn't know her very well.
Now it was almost over, and pleasant enough.
In my mind I gave thanks to the woodpecker,

who couldn't seem to decide where to stash his
    quarry.
Then Anne fixed me, one eye magnified behind her
    glasses,
What are your plans for him?
Meaning my father, in the bed between us.

He played along, gave no indication
that either of us was there, staring out the door
at the woodpecker. I said recovery first,
then assisted living, maybe, *I don't know, we'll have
    to see.*

Going out, in the hallway she was far enough ahead,
I could have just let her go. But that felt wrong:
she was my dad's friend, she had brought the
    birdseed,
we had watched the woodpecker together.

I called out to her, thanked her for coming.
She turned and took my measure
through her looking glass.
I never thought it would come to this.

I allowed myself her accusation: acorn forced into a tree.
I was to blame for the decision he had made,
from which everything had gone wrong,
as she'd known it would.

My Mother in Fall

The night before, she was at her desk,
working on the same scholarly book
she'd been writing since I was in high school,
on Henry James, the New York Edition,
and what both he and she called his "case,"
an argument requiring labyrinthine syntax
that could strand even an expert reader.
My father, the editor, the Thoreauvian, counseled
   simplicity.
Her objection: that would not be accurate.

Several times that evening, he called her to bed.
"I *have* to finish this," he said she said.
As if she knew, or maybe by the time they left the
   house
in the early morning dark for the airport
and the flight east, that she would not
sit down again at that desk, concentration rising
with smoke from her cigarette.

How far did she get? Did she make it over the Sierras,
the Nevada desert? Somewhere before the prairie
she had crossed so many times,
the vessel burst into her brain,
the leaf that blows ahead of the season.

Overpass

Two days after
my mother died
I lay on the mat
in the storefront studio
down the street from the tracks.

My mother appeared
at the top of the overpass.
I waited for her
to come closer,
but she stopped,
as if this was as far
as she was allowed to go.

She gave me the look
I'd seen many times before
when she needed to leave.

I started crying
as silently as I could.
I didn't want anyone
to know, or ask questions.

Down the steps,
crickets balanced
on basement walls.

Grass

It grows easily, everywhere,
not always the way we want.

We bring in soil to even out the dips,
spread new seed while the weather's temperate.

Weeds blow, seed in.
Onion grass and ground ivy are bad influences.

Cut it too short, the roots won't sustain
when it gets hot and dry.

Let it grow and it will be wild,
not fit for get-togethers or barbecues.

Everyone's a critic, whether they say so or not.
How well have we tended our creation?

Have we neglected what we should have dealt with?
Have we over-fertilized?

One midsummer afternoon,
passing more quickly than we could have thought,

it will shine green and lush until twilight,
drawing on the earth where it is planted.

May we live to see it.

Eighteen Lines for a Young Life

News moves through the neighborhood,
parent to parent, whispering details
not spoken in the message from the principal.
A boy plays in the band,
the flute sestet at the chamber music concert.
He graduates on Thursday.
His family throws a party on Saturday.
Sunday morning, he hangs himself.
Voted most likely to become a superhero,
missing from the yearbook "due to saving the world."
Did that make him feel like flying?
Or remind him of the hardness below?
Did he think to heave himself outside this world
as if pulling himself through a window?
Solution with nothing left over.
If I found my child blue and lifeless,
I would tear the clothes from my body,
drag fingernails through my skin.

Untitled

The sea is a room without walls. It spills, falling over land. Land shears away into sea, rooms echo with spills and falling walls. Walls are powerless in the war of land and water, swells uproot trees, sweep cars, shopping carts, diamond necklaces out to sea, rooms of plastic ingots drifting down. The sea has room, gathering spoils from falling lands.

North Pacific

I.
When trapped under ropes or suspended in ice,
seawater may seep through imperfections;
when the netting wears off, its pattern may remain.

II.
Fishermen's floats blown from sake bottles
turn in the North Pacific:
Japan to Alaska to California,
and back across the Pacific.

II.
Breaking free on storms or tides,
some wash up on beaches of Taiwan,
Canada, and the northwest U.S.
They have been found in coral reefs
on the windward side of Guam.
A few are stuck in the Arctic ice pack.
It is believed that floats washing up in Alaska
have spent seven to ten years in the gyre,
that most have been afloat longer than that.

IV.
The ones my mother hung
in the window of our old apartment
were replicas, most likely from Cost Plus.
Decanted sea colors of early childhood,
blue and green currents of family life,
bubbles and streaks in uneven glass.

In Winter

After the college tour,
my son asks what it's like in winter.
We are looking out over Lake Champlain,
in short sleeves, having eaten lunch in a repurposed garage,
bay doors rolled up to let the outdoors in.
Long, my husband and I say at the same time.
There's a lot of snow, we say, though we know he knows that
much, and in any case, no place gets the snowfalls
of our childhoods anymore.
It snows in May, my husband says, *but it melts pretty fast.*

Across the water—impossible that this could freeze,
dark blue and untroubled as clarified sky—
a sightseeing boat decked in party lights
moves steadily toward us.
How to transmit the knowledge
we grew up with?

To tell the truth, we've gotten used
to where we are living now,
and the memory dims within us.

Pressing the brake impertinently,
radio blaring into the drift,
I slide across the whitened road
so slowly it could take seventeen years.

To My Son

If I could, I would crawl inside you and curl up like a
    dog.
Last night I dreamed you were in some sort of trouble.
I was trying to help, not doing any good.
How to translate what's in the space between
    my heart and stomach?
The thing you put there.
Yesterday somebody asked me the name of a tree.
I wanted to answer. She had chosen me to ask.
She broke off the end of a branch
to show someone else.
Leaves lined up on both sides of the stem.
I recognized the shape, and still no name.
I am crossing a desert.
You are crossing a sea.

Flatirons

From anywhere in the city so close
look up and there they are,
intimate, as if you could press
against the chalky slabs,
red-brown rising from crush of pines:
Flatirons.

No mystery to the name: heavy triangles of iron
used to smother wrinkles out of clothes.
They imprint, so one might reasonably pine
for them after even a few short hours.
Sheared-off slabs
grow smaller in the rearview as we press on.

Flatirons press
Tower slabs
Close pines

Calls

1. *Fridays*

After his wife got sick, when he still had his own lab,
late Friday afternoons we used to talk
in the hour before I had to pick up my son from aftercare.
I'd look out the window: slanting light, the copper beech.
When his voice dropped away and I couldn't hear,
I stayed on, as I had years ago, late at night in our dorms,
talked until I was sick of talking, not wanting to hang up.
This wasn't just on my side. We both had a hard time
disengaging, our voices making another circle as our time
    wore out
and I had to run out to the car and hope to beat traffic,
a lingering I never experienced like that with anyone else.

2. *Father*

This is your dad, bellowed into the phone,
sometimes prefaced with *Bonjour!*
Identification hardly necessary, clear from the first syllable.
Sunday nights. Always in the middle of something, I was,
no matter how I tried to avoid it, getting ready for the week
    ahead.
Growing up, when my mother told him to lower his voice
on the phone to my grandmother,
he'd say *I have to shout all the way to California.*
When my mother fell asleep on an airplane
and couldn't be woken up,
I came home from evening work, late.
The phone rang. *I can't do it, I'm just too tired,* I said.
You have to take this, my husband said,
pressing the receiver into my hands.

3. Son

Better to text or FaceTime.
His chin has a tendency
to drift, taking his voice with it,
pointing out to the world,
not into a microphone.
*I can't hear you, honey,
can you speak into the phone?*
I *am,* I *am,* he insists
and the conversation ends
in a swirl of familial annoyance.
His long man's face appears in the screen,
Colorado sky behind him,
free of particulate.

Letter to the Sky

Across our bowl
deep as our atmosphere,
you provide friction for those attempting re-entry.

Clouds are garments you put on and discard.
You layer them up and peel them off.
When you fling them
they scoop us up and hurl down on us.

I saw your bare chest once
on a late summer evening in northern Canada,
your salmon ribs as you lazed above the landscape.

I don't know why I thought of winter then,
how impossible when enmeshed in one
it is to imagine another.

I tried to see the lake frozen over, updrafts of snow,
you bundled in a thick gray coat, turning away.

Do you get tired of people staring at you?
Do you like the attention?

We parse you for clues as to what is to happen.
Once predictions are made, we ignore them.

Practice

The small precision:
word matched to moment,
finger placed squarely on the string,
the pitch containing not only itself,
but itself halved, and that halved, and again.
Ratios that move the small bones of the ear
translate resonance to brain.
Lives of sloppy shifts, wrong notes,
mistakes in tonality.

Late at night in the living room,
try to make up for these.
In your notebook, on the instrument, with a partner,
practice harmony, or necessary dissonance,
half-step leading tones.

Branch

Falls across my window like a sprig in a Japanese
    vase.
Last summer's leaves, cured light tobacco, folded like
    petals.
All winter they've remained, drape suspended.
Twenty-three winters I've looked out this window.
I do not remember seeing old leaves hold on like this.
Perhaps I am forgetful or never bothered to notice.
Within a month buds will appear and with their
    swelling what happens?
Will the dead leaves drop one by one or all at
    once? Either way, will I notice?
Are they crowded out by new growth?
I stare out the window when I am stuck or thinking.
Leaves dark in May turn green in August, yellow in
    November.
In September we sweep the patio of puckered casings,
relieved of their nuts by squirrels.
The branch holding words I am trying to form.

The Cup

Too hot to drink in the beginning.
With time a skin, puckered at the sides,
grew across the top.

I ran a spoon around the inside edge.
It hung against the silver
like the pelt of a small brown animal.

I put down the spoon, lifted the stoneware
to my lips, let in a sip,
coating my tongue and the roof of my mouth.

Sweetness and acidity
a half step removed from burning,
tang of fruit.

It keeps its secrets well,
layered and evaporating.

Already as I drank the heat was draining off.
What warmth could be captured flowed into my chest,
joining my own, traveling out.

Understanding

Earth is waiting & ready to soak up
what the day sends down

The sky is waiting for wind
blows clouds across its face

Wind races across the face of earth
coming around on the other side

Ocean waits for pull of tides

Leaves wait for light to open
roots for water they will ferry up

Blossoms open to insect feet
& from that teasing form the fruit

Day stretches tired in the afternoon

Spring waits for summer
summer for fall
falls into a blanket of winter

Underground waits for thaw
feeds on root sugar & grows

Rivers wait to rise return to sea

Days can be counted but what sets off movement
down the canal

Young wait to pull sense from sounds
in the waiting repeat them

Later they will make their own
using palate tongue teeth & lips

& waiting still for something else
burrowing to ground

Slipped between passing clouds
sucked up through roots to bloom

Notes

"Poem Ending with Lines from Samuel Beckett"—Lines from Beckett's short story, "The Expelled," 1948.

"Oneself"—Refers to events related in the film *Adrift* (Simon & Schuster, 2018), produced and directed by Baltasar Kormákur and written by David Branson Smith, Aaron Kandell and Jordan Kandell, based on a true story that occurred in 1983.

"Margaret Atwood in Quarantine"—Inspired by the novels of The MaddAddam Trilogy, *Oryx and Crake* (2003), *Year of the Flood* (2009), and *MaddAddam* (2013), in which a man-made virus, the brainchild of a brilliant but disturbed young man, is spread through pharmaceuticals with the aim of allowing newly-engineered beings to take the place of humans. The novels were written and published before the advent of the Covid-19 virus, which emerged without the aid of genetic engineering.

"*Buciumeana*"—The fourth of six movements in Béla Bartók's *Rumanian Folk Dances for Small Orchestra*, originally composed for piano in 1915 and orchestrated for small ensemble in 1917. The movement is named for the Bucsony region (today Bucuim, Alba County) in Romania.

"Bartók in America"—Serge Koussevitsky, music director of the Boston Symphony Orchestra from 1924-1949, commissioned the piece that became known as "Concerto for Orchestra" from Bartók, premiered in December 1944. Bartók died in 1945 at age 64 in New York from complications of leukemia. Upon his death, Bartók left two unfinished works, *Piano Concerto #3*, which was only missing some orchestration, and *Viola*

Concerto, for which the viola part had been completed and the orchestral part only sketchily scored.

"Knowing Is a Branching Trail that Disappears into Variety"—Quotation is from Darwin's *Origin of the Species*. For information and speculation about Ediacarans, I am indebted to Robert Moor's fascinating and original book *Trails: An Exploration* (Simon & Schuster, 2016).

"Twin"—This poem is not only about a duplex, or twin, home, but is a poetic duplex, a form created by Jericho Brown, in which the first line of each couplet mirrors the second line of the previous couplet, and the final line mirrors the opening. In a blog post initially published in April 2019 and republished in May 2020 on the Poetry Foundation website, Brown writes, "I decided to call the form a duplex because something about its repetition and its couplets made me feel like it was a house with two addresses . . . I wanted to highlight the trouble of a wall between us who live within a single structure." (https://www.poetryfoundation.org/harriet-books/2020/05/invention) Horsehair plaster was a common technique for building interior walls from the turn of the century through WWII. The plaster is composed of lime, aggregate and water, and dries (or "cures") by absorbing atmospheric carbon and carbonates. Horsehair was added for structural strength. Application requires three layers applied to wood lath with spacing $3/8$ to $1/2$ inch apart. When the first "scratch coat" is pressed against the lath, the plaster is squeezed through the holes between the lath, and the excess on the other side forms "keys" that wrap around the lath, holding the wall in place. After WWII, the advent of gypsum drywall panels made the construction of interior walls much less labor-intensive and time-consuming.

"Who Is Right About Moonlight?"—Ryōkan Taigu (1758-1831) was a poet and Soto Zen Buddhist monk who lived most of his life as a hermit. Among the many stories told about him is the time that Ryōkan caught a thief in his hut, and, since there was nothing there to steal, immediately took off his clothes, and gave them to the man so he would not go away empty-handed. As the thief retreated, Ryōkan regretted that he could not give him the moon (a frequent symbol of enlightenment in Zen Buddhism). The story may relate to one of Ryōkan's haiku. Izumi Shikibu (born 976?) was a mid-Heian period Japanese poet, member of the Thirty-Six Medieval Poetry Immortals. She is the author of the haiku "Although the wind," translated by Jane Hirshfield and Mariko Aritani: "Although the wind/blows terribly here,/the moon-light also leaks/between the roof planks/of this ruined house" (*The Ink-Dark Moon: Love Poems by Onono Komacki and Izumi Shikibu, Women of the Ancient Court of Japan*, Knopf, 1988).

"The Aurochs"—References the cave paintings of Lascaux, France.

"St. Peter's Shadow"—In Acts 5:15 in the Christian Bible, St. Peter is able to cure the sick if his shadow but touches them. Many are acquainted with the story through the fresco by the Florentine artist Masaccio (1401-1428).

About the Author

Alison Hicks is the author of poetry collections *You Who Took the Boat Out* and *Kiss*, a chapbook *Falling Dreams*, and a novella *Love: A Story of Images.* Her work has appeared in *Eclipse, Gargoyle, Permafrost*, and *Poet Lore,* among other journals. She was named a finalist for the 2021 Beullah Rose Prize by *Smartish Pace*; was nominated for a Pushcart Prize by *Green Hills Literary Lantern;* and has received two fellowships from the Pennsylvania Council of the Arts. She graduated *summa cum laude* from Bryn Mawr College, and holds an MFA from the University of Arizona. In 1996, she founded Greater Philadelphia Wordshop Studio to support writers in the development of their individual voices and practice of their craft through community-based workshops and private consultation. With Elizabeth Mosier and Therése Halscheid, she co-edited *Prompted*, an anthology of work from the first 13 years of the Wordshop Studio. She lives in Havertown, PA with her husband, Charles Greifenstein.

www.philawordshop.com

Acknowledgments

I would like to thank Leonard Gontarek and the Saturday Osage Poets, who saw early drafts of these poems; Trudy Hale of The Porches Writing Retreat, where this book was first put together; and Catherine Bancroft, who offered comments and helpful guidance on that first draft of the book. Though I have mentioned the references more specifically in the notes, I want to recognize here the writers, artists, and thinkers whose work I drew shamelessly upon in composing many of these poems: Charles Darwin, Samuel Beckett, Bela Bartók, Margaret Atwood, Jane Hirshfield, Robert Moor, Ryōken Taigu, Izumi Shikibu, Jericho Brown, Baltasar Kormákur, Masaccio, and the anonymous painters of the Lascaux caves.

My heart overflows with gratitude to Huascar Medina for selecting my work for the 2021 Birdy Prize. I am indeed blessed to work with Tracy Million Simmons and Meadowlark Press. Located on the edge of what remains of the Tallgrass Prairie, Meadowlark represents the best of what small presses have to offer their region, the country, and the world, cultivating and helping to sustain a cultural ecosystem. Thanks also to Linzi Garcia at Meadowlark for her energy and enthusiasm, Amy Small-McKinney for her friendship and sharing of poems, and finally, my husband Charles Greifenstein, and my son, Jeremy Greifenstein, for putting up with my seeming inability to estimate time and my perpetual lateness for dinner, and for being part of this continuing journey.

Publication Credits

I am deeply grateful to the publications in which the following poems appeared, or are forthcoming, sometimes in slightly different form:

Alexandria Quarterly, "To My Son"

Blood Orange Review, "The Moon Is a Paper Lantern, Arm of the Boy Who Carries It Tired," "Yellow Bird"

Boomer LitMag, "The Aurochs," "Pain in the Neck"

Cleaver Magazine, "How It Is"

Cloudbank, "Poem Ending with Lines by Samuel Beckett"

Common Ground Review, "My Mother in Fall"

DASH, "Bartók," "Bartók in America"

Door is a Jar, "Sea Otter," "Grass"

Drunk Monkeys, "Boat"

East Jasmine Review, "St. Peter's Shadow"

ELM Literary Magazine, "Knowing Is a Branching Trail that Disappears into Variety," "North Pacific"

Evening Street Review, "The IV Pole"

Green Hills Literary Lantern, "Color"

Jelly Bucket, "Migraineurs"

Magnolia Review, "Island," "From a Prescribed Distance," "An Open Door Is an Invitation in the Same Way as a Closed Box," "Branch," "Understanding"

Muddy River Poetry Review, "Groundwater"

Paperplates, "Walking the Dog I," "Walking the Dog II"

Packingtown Review Journal, "Suites for Solo Cello, May 2020"

Penman Review, "Westland House"

Pioneertown, "Katydids & Cicadas," "Flatirons"

Plainsongs, "In Winter"

Poet Lore, "Starlings"

Sheila-Na-Gig Online, "Calls"

Straight Forward Poetry, "Oakmont"

Summerset Review, "Landscape with Citrus"

Vagabond City, "Letter to the Sky"

Vending Machine Press, "Overpass"

The Virginia Normal, "Sunflower"

Vox Poetica, "The Pelicans," "Riffles," "The Winter Magician"

Wrath-Bearing Tree, "Untitled"

Publication Credits

I am deeply grateful to the publications in which the following poems appeared, or are forthcoming, sometimes in slightly different form:

Alexandria Quarterly, "To My Son"

Blood Orange Review, "The Moon Is a Paper Lantern, Arm of the Boy Who Carries It Tired," "Yellow Bird"

Boomer LitMag, "The Aurochs," "Pain in the Neck"

Cleaver Magazine, "How It Is"

Cloudbank, "Poem Ending with Lines by Samuel Beckett"

Common Ground Review, "My Mother in Fall"

DASH, "Bartók," "Bartók in America"

Door is a Jar, "Sea Otter," "Grass"

Drunk Monkeys, "Boat"

East Jasmine Review, "St. Peter's Shadow"

ELM Literary Magazine, "Knowing Is a Branching Trail that Disappears into Variety," "North Pacific"

Evening Street Review, "The IV Pole"

Green Hills Literary Lantern, "Color"

Jelly Bucket, "Migraineurs"

Magnolia Review, "Island," "From a Prescribed Distance," "An Open Door Is an Invitation in the Same Way as a Closed Box," "Branch," "Understanding"

Muddy River Poetry Review, "Groundwater"

Paperplates, "Walking the Dog I," "Walking the Dog II"

Packingtown Review Journal, "Suites for Solo Cello, May 2020"

Penman Review, "Westland House"

Pioneertown, "Katydids & Cicadas," "Flatirons"

Plainsongs, "In Winter"

Poet Lore, "Starlings"

Sheila-Na-Gig Online, "Calls"

Straight Forward Poetry, "Oakmont"

Summerset Review, "Landscape with Citrus"

Vagabond City, "Letter to the Sky"

Vending Machine Press, "Overpass"

The Virginia Normal, "Sunflower"

Vox Poetica, "The Pelicans," "Riffles," "The Winter Magician"

Wrath-Bearing Tree, "Untitled"

Meadowlark POETRY

Books are a way to explore, connect, and discover. Poetry incites us to observe and think in new ways, bridging our understanding of the world with our artistic need to interact with, shape, and share it with others.

Publishing poetry is our way of saying—

*We love these words,
we want to preserve them,
we want to play a role in sharing them
with the world.*

www.birdypoetryprize.com

Meadowlark Press created The Birdy Poetry Prize to celebrate the voices of our era. Cash prize, publication, and 50 copies awarded annually.

The Birdy is an annual competition.

Final Deadline for Entries: December 1, midnight.

Entry Fee: $25

All entries will be considered for standard Meadowlark Press publishing contract offers, as well.

Full-length poetry manuscripts (55 page minimum) will be considered. Poems may be previously published in journals and/or anthologies, but not in full-length, single-author volumes. All poets are eligible to enter, regardless of publishing history.

See www.birdypoetryprize.com for complete submission guidelines. Also visit us at meadowlark-books.com.

www.ingramcontent.com/pod-product-compliance
Lightning Source LLC
Chambersburg PA
CBHW020037120526
44589CB00032B/577